The Adventures of Hercules

Written by I. M. Richardson
Illustrated by Robert Baxter

Troll Associates

Library of Congress Cataloging in Publication Data

Richardson, I. M.
    The adventures of Hercules.

    Summary: Hercules, son of the god Zeus and a mortal
woman, renowned for his great strength, performs
twelve dangerous tasks to atone for an attack on
his wife and children.
    1. Hercules (Roman mythology)—Juvenile litera-
ture. [1. Hercules (Roman mythology) 2. Mythology,
Greek] I. Baxter, Robert, 1930-   ill. II. Title.
BL820.H5R53 1983   292'.213   82-16557
ISBN 0-89375-865-5
ISBN 0-89375-866-3 (pbk.)

The Ancient Greeks had many great heroes. But the greatest hero of all was half god and half man. His Greek name was Heracles, but he is better known by his Roman name— Hercules.

Hercules received his strength from his father. His father was Zeus, the most powerful of all the gods on Mount Olympus. But his mother was a mortal. This annoyed the goddess Hera, who was Zeus's wife, and made her very jealous.

Soon after he was born, Hera tried to kill Hercules. She sent two deadly snakes into his room. But Hercules seized one snake in each hand and strangled them both. His mother did not know what to think of this. So she went to the blind prophet of Thebes, who said, "Hercules shall become a hero to all people."

When he was still very young, Hercules was sent into the
mountains. There, he worked as a shepherd boy. One day, a
lion crept out of the forest, looking for a meal. Hercules fought
the beast and killed it with his bare hands.

From that time on, he wore the skin of the lion as a hood and cloak. He also made a huge club that was so heavy that no one could lift it off the ground. But Hercules could swing it around as easily as if it were a thin stick.

By the time he had grown up, Hercules was the strongest man on earth. In battle, his great strength and courage made him unbeatable. He once helped King Creon of Thebes defeat the armies of a neighboring king. Soon afterward, Hercules married Creon's daughter, Megara. They had three children and were very happy.

But the jealous goddess Hera had sworn that she would make Hercules suffer. One day, she caused him to attack his wife and children. When he regained his senses and realized what he had done, Hercules was overcome with grief. "How can I ever live with this terrible pain and guilt?" he cried.

The Oracle at Delphi often answered difficult questions for the Greeks. Hercules went to the Oracle and asked how he could cleanse himself of his sins. The Oracle replied, "You must go to Mycenae and serve King Eurystheus for twelve years. Only by doing this will you ever be free of your pain and guilt."

So Hercules made the journey to Mycenae. King Eurystheus could hardly believe his luck—the strongest man in the world wanted to be his servant! At once, he began thinking of difficult tasks for Hercules. Hera secretly helped the king. Together, they thought of twelve dangerous tasks, which came to be called the labors of Hercules.

The first labor was to kill the lion of Nemea. For years, this great beast had terrorized the valley to the north. First, Hercules tried to shoot it with his arrows. But the lion's skin was so tough that the arrows bounced off! So he took his club and struck the lion until it was dazed. Finally, Hercules seized the lion and strangled it with his bare hands.

He tossed the dead lion over his shoulder and returned to the city. When Eurystheus saw the huge beast, he realized for the first time just how strong and powerful Hercules was. From then on, the king kept a safe distance between himself and the mighty son of Zeus.

The second task for Hercules was to overcome the Hydra. This snake-like monster lived in a nearby swamp. It had nine heads, and one of them could never die. The other eight were special in a different way—if one of them was cut off, two more heads would grow in its place! At first, this task seemed impossible, even for Hercules.

14

But he soon found a way to keep the Hydra from growing new heads. Each time he cut off one of the old heads, he immediately closed the wound by burning it with a fiery stick. Then he rolled a heavy rock onto the head that would not die. Before he returned to Mycenae, Hercules dipped each of his arrows into the Hydra's deadly poison.

The next labor of Hercules was to find the stag with golden horns, and bring it back alive. This golden deer was sacred to the goddess Artemis. Hercules followed the stag through the forests for a whole year. Finally, he captured it and brought it back alive. The goddess did not stop him, because she knew he would not keep the golden stag.

The fourth labor was to capture a wild boar that had terrorized the people on the mountainside. The boar was huge and ugly, with sharply pointed tusks, and short, stubby legs. Hercules chased it high up the mountain, where it became trapped in a deep snowbank. Then he subdued the beast and carried it off to Mycenae.

The fifth labor of Hercules was to clean the Augean stables in a single day. This may not sound like a difficult task, but these stables were the home of thousands of cattle. And the stables had not been cleaned in thirty years! Using his great strength, Hercules changed the course of two rivers, and the rushing waters washed the stables clean.

The next task Hercules had to perform was to destroy the Stymphalian birds. These man-eating creatures had brass claws and brass beaks. They hid in the thickets near the black waters of the Stymphalian Lake. The goddess Athena helped Hercules drive the birds out of their hiding places with a special rattle. Then Hercules shot them with his poisoned arrows.

Half the labors of Hercules had now been completed. But six more tasks lay ahead, before the son of Zeus would be free of pain and guilt. King Eurystheus said, "There is a savage bull on the island of Crete. Capture it, and bring it to me." Before long, Hercules had set sail for Crete.

When he arrived on the island, Hercules found the bull destroying the countryside. People ran in terror when it came near. But Hercules seized the bull and wrestled it to the ground. Then he slung it over his shoulders and carried it off. When he brought it to Eurystheus, the King quickly sent him off on another difficult labor.

This time, Hercules had to capture the man-eating mares. They
belonged to Diomedes, the King of Thrace. To travel to Thrace
was a dangerous journey, for any strangers were tossed to the
mares, who instantly tore them apart.

22

There were four mares, and they were always hungry. Even if Hercules could grasp two—one in each hand—the other two would attack him and tear him apart. But the son of Zeus had a plan. He seized the wicked King Diomedes and tossed him to the man-eating mares. The animals soon became so tame that Hercules could lead them back to Mycenae.

To complete his ninth labor, Hercules had to go to the country of the Amazons, a tribe of fierce warrior women. Their queen, Hippolyta, wore a beautiful golden belt. The daughter of Eurystheus wanted it, and Hercules was told to get it. Hippolyta willingly gave the golden belt to the mighty Hercules. But again, jealous Hera interfered.

Disguised as an Amazon, the goddess began to stir up trouble.
"He will take our queen from us," she whispered. "We must
stop him!" Then the warrior women attacked Hercules and
tried to kill him. But he was more powerful than even an army
of Amazons. He fought them off and returned to Mycenae
with the golden belt.

Next, Hercules had to capture the cattle of the monster called Geryon. Geryon lived on an island, where his cattle were guarded by a giant and a two-headed dog. After Hercules killed the guards, the monster himself arrived. There was a long and bitter fight, but when it was over, Hercules had slain Geryon. At last, he started home with the cattle.

When Hercules stopped to rest, a fire-breathing giant made off with some of the cattle. But the son of Zeus discovered where they were hidden, and he went to get them back. Suddenly, the giant rushed out of a rocky cave, and there was a mighty battle. But in the end, the giant was slain, and Hercules continued home.

For his eleventh labor, Hercules was told to get the golden apples of the Hesperides. The Hesperides were three nymphs who watched the apples for the goddess, Hera. They were assisted by a many-headed dragon, who would attack anyone who dared to pick the apples. The Hesperides were the daughters of Atlas, the god who held the weight of the skies on his shoulders. So Hercules asked Atlas to help him.

"If you will hold up the sky," Atlas replied, "I will get the apples." So Hercules took the weight upon his own shoulders. When Atlas returned with the apples, he did not want his job back. But Hercules tricked him. "Take back this weight for only a moment," he said. "I want to make a pad to ease the burden on my shoulders." Then, when he was rid of the burden, Hercules took the golden apples and left.

The twelfth labor of Hercules was to bring back Cerberus—the terrible three-headed watchdog of the dead. Hercules had to pass through the dark tunnel that led down to the lower world. The King of the Dead gave him permission to take Cerberus away, as long as Hercules did not use any weapons. He would have to fight the horrible beast with his bare hands!

Cerberus stood guarding the gates of the kingdom of the dead. His three heads snarled viciously as Hercules approached. But the snarling stopped when Hercules seized the watchdog by two of his throats, and slowly squeezed them. Then Hercules lifted the beast high overhead and returned to Mycenae. When Eurystheus saw the watchdog of the dead, he begged Hercules to take him back where he had come from.

And so, the twelve labors of Hercules were completed. The son of Zeus had rid the world of hideous beasts and terrible monsters. He had done brave and mighty deeds that no other person had ever done or would ever do again. The words of the blind prophet of Thebes had come true. Hercules had become the hero of all people.